# Practise Number Skills

Colour each picture as you finish each page.

*Written by Jillian Harker and Geraldine Taylor*
*Illustrated by John Dillow*

# Counting to 10

Welcome to Addington.
Everyone here likes numbers and sums.

Nicky Number is counting the creatures in his garden.
Can you help him fill in his list?

How many?

cats

birds

frogs

spiders

beetles

worms

butterflies

ants

bees

ladybirds

_____
_____
_____
_____
_____
_____
_____
_____
_____
_____

Nicky's sister, Naomi Number, collects things to count. Draw a line to help her match each collection to its label.

## Try your skills

Fill in the missing numbers.

1 2 ☐ 4 5 6 ☐ 8 9 ☐

Put a circle round the bigger number,
like this ⑧ or 1.    4 or 6    7 or 3    9 or 5 or 2

**Parent point:** Children enjoy counting things they see around them. Encourage every opportunity to do this.

# Estimation & checking

George Guess and Charlie Check are friends.
They play number games around the town.
See how they play.

Now you can join in.
How many?

| | Look and Guess | Count and Check |
|---|---|---|
| | | |
| | | |
| | | |
| | | |
| | | |
| | | |
| | | |
| | | |
| | | |
| | | |
| | | |

## Try your skills

Play this game with your family at home.

*Check it out!*

**Parent point:** Estimation and checking for accuracy are vital maths skills. Make this into a game at home using buttons, counters and other objects.

# Addition to 10

Terri and Trudy Total are twins.

They are helping their mother to take orders in her café.

Help them to add up the orders.

Draw and write how many altogether.

| 2 | + | 1 | = | 3 |

☐ + ☐ = ☐

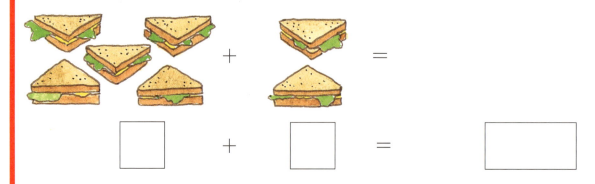

☐ + ☐ = ☐

☐ + ☐ = ☐

Now you can do these café sums. Write the answers in the picture.

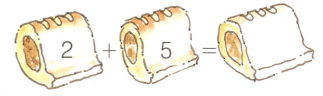
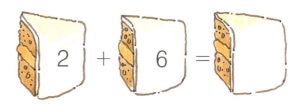

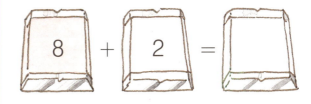

## Try your skills

Sums can be written like this
3 + 2 = 5
or like this

Can you do these?

4 + 3 = ☐   6 +
              1 +
              ___

**Parent point:** Make sure your child is given lots of opportunities to add using real objects.

# Subtraction to 10

Mr Minus owns the town's take away food shop. Help him work out how much food he has left.

There are 6 cartons of fries.
The customers take away 2 cartons.
How many are left?

| 6 | – | 2 | = | 4 |

There are ___ cartons of curry.
The customer takes away ___ carton.
How many are left?

There are ___ packs of sandwiches.
The customers take away ___ packs.
How many are left?

Can you do these take aways (subtractions)?
Write your answer on the pictures.

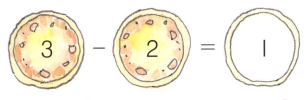

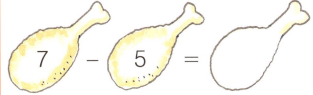

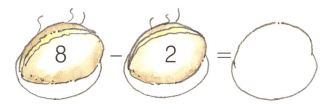

## Try your skills

Subtractions can be written like this
6 – 3 = 3
or like this

```
  6
-
  3
─────
  3
```

Can you do these?

7 – 2 = ☐

```
  7
-
  2
─────
```

**Parent point:** Children will hear different terms being used for the same calculation. Help by using the words subtraction, take away and minus when you are doing these sums together.

Can you fill in the tens and units for these?

## Try your skills

5 tens and 2 units is the same as 52.

Now you try these.

1 ten and 3 units is the same as  _____

7 tens and 6 units is the same as  _____

**Parent point:** Plenty of practice at grouping objects (buttons, counters, etc) will help your child to understand place value. This means that the position of a number tells you how much it is worth. For example, in 67 the 6 is worth 6 lots of ten and the 7 is worth 7 single units.

# Fractions, halves & quarters

Flora Fraction runs the food stall at Addington Festival. She needs to cut her cakes in half ready to sell.

Draw a line through the middle to show her where to cut them.

These need to be cut in quarters. Draw 2 lines to show where.

This food must be divided in half to go onto two plates, with the same amount on each.

Half of 4 is 2.

Now share this food between 2 plates.
Draw a line and write the numbers on the plates.

Half of 6 is _____

Half of 8 is _____

Now share this food into quarters to go onto 4 plates.

Draw lines and write the numbers on the plates.

A quarter of 4 is _____

A quarter of 8 is _____

**Parent point:** Have lots of family fun sharing things. Involve children in dividing things into halves and quarters, or into groups of twos and fours.

# The concept of Zero

Zero the conjuror is giving a magic show at the festival.
He is making things disappear.

George holds out 6 marbles.
Zero makes them all disappear.
There are none left.

6 – 6 = 0

What happens when Zero does these tricks?
Write the calculation.

Naomi is wearing 8 rosettes.
Zero makes them all disappear.

☐ – ☐ = ☐

Terry and Trudy are wearing 2 paper hats.
Zero makes them both disappear.

☐ – ☐ = ☐

Charlie was too late for the show.
He has 3 juggling balls. Zero has made none disappear.
Can you write the calculation?

☐ – ☐ = ☐

Zero has another trick.
He can make things come back again.

| 0 | + | 2 | = | 2 |

Your turn to write the calculation.

| ☐ | + | ☐ | = | ☐ |

| ☐ | + | ☐ | = | ☐ |

## Try your skills

Can you work these out?

0 + 4 = ☐      2 − 0 = ☐

3 + 0 = ☐      3 − 3 = ☐

6 + 0 = ☐      5 − 5 = ☐

0 + 1 = ☐      9 − 0 = ☐

I have 8 rosettes — there are 0 more to bring back. 8 + 0 = 8

Nothing to it!

**Parent point:** Understanding the idea of nothing in number is a basic skill. Play vanishing tricks like this and then make objects reappear. Vary the language you use. Nothing can also be called zero, nought and nil.

# Addition to 20

Albert Adder is running the winning ticket game.

12 + 8 = 20

The winning tickets add up to 20. Draw a ★ on all the winning tickets.

- 2 + 16 =
- 4 + 16 =
- 0 + 11 =
- 7 + 7 =
- 18 + 2 =
- 10 + 10 =
- 3 + 6 =
- 5 + 8 =
- 12 + 3 =
- 8 + 8 =
- 18 + 1 =
- 5 + 6 =
- 4 + 2 =
- 15 + 5 =

Can you fill in the missing numbers on these tickets?

1 + 12 =

11 + 9 =

7 + 4 =

5 + 7 =

9 + 3 =

3 + 13 =

20 + 0 =

6 + 6 =

13 + 7 =

It all adds up!

## Try your skills

17 + ☐ = 20

9 + ☐ = 20

0 + ☐ = 20

☐ + 5 = 20

**Parent point:** Knowing the pairs of numbers (number bonds) which add to make 20 is very important. Help your child to see the patterns:
eg      6 + 4 = 10      7 + 3 = 10
        16 + 4 = 20     17 + 3 = 20

# Using money & subtraction to 20

Penny Cost is at the town festival. She has a bag of 20p coins.

How much will she spend if she buys

two turns on the 'Hoopla' ☐

three turns on the 'Try your strength' ☐

one turn on the 'Hoopla' and one turn at 'Name the teddy' ☐

one turn on 'Try your strength' and one turn on 'Winning numbers' ☐

one turn at 'Face painting' and one turn at the 'Lucky dip'? ☐

## Try your skills

Now Penny has only 20p left.
How much change will she get if she spends

5p on a 'Lucky dip'  20p − 5p = ☐

15p on a 'Winning number' ticket  20p − 15p = ☐

8p on 'Try your strength'  20p − 8p = ☐

4p on 'Name the teddy'  20p − 4p = ☐

10p on the 'Hoopla'  20p − 10p = ☐

20p on 'Face painting'?  20p − 20p = ☐

*Every penny counts.*

**Parent point:** Provide plenty of opportunities for your child to shop and handle money.

# Multiplication tables

Tom Times grows fruit and vegetables to sell in Addington. He packs them in rows in boxes. He needs your help to work out how many things he will have to sell.

5 + 5 + 5 = 15

3 lots of 5 make 15

3 x 5 = 15

2 + 2 + 2 + 2 + 2 + 2 = ☐

6 lots of 2 make ☐

6 x 2 = ☐

Now help with these.

3 lots of 4 = ☐

3 x 4 = ☐

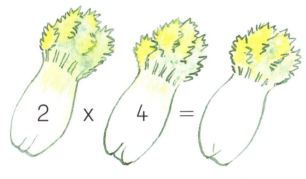

2 x 4 =

5 x 3 =

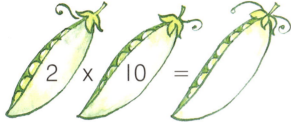

2 x 10 =

8 x 2 =

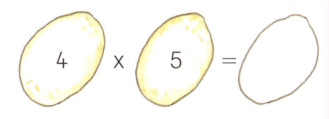

4 x 5 =

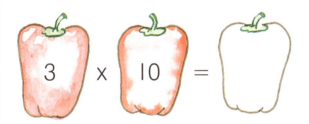

3 x 10 =

*Right every time!*

## Try your skills

Can you do these?

7 x 2 = ☐     5 x 2 = ☐     4 x 6 = ☐

6 x 3 = ☐     7 x 10 = ☐    3 x 7 = ☐

7 x 5 = ☐     3 x 8 = ☐     4 x 3 = ☐

**Parent point:** Use buttons or counters laid out in rows to help your child understand tables calculations. Ladybird's **Learn Times Tables** will help you.

# Time and measurement

Mr Minute is the clockmaker.
He likes to be on time.
Draw the hands on his clocks to show his daily timetable.

three o'clock

seven o'clock

half past eight

ten o'clock

half past twelve

quarter past three    half past five

Miss Measure is the school nurse. Today she is weighing and measuring the school children.

Please fill in their charts for her.

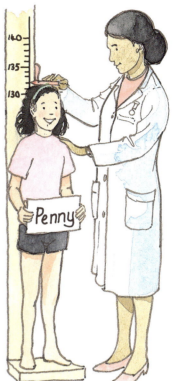

| | Penny |
|---|---|
| Height | ....................cm |
| Weight | ....................kg |

| | Nicky |
|---|---|
| Height | ....................cm |
| Weight | ....................kg |

| | Charlie |
|---|---|
| Height | ....................cm |
| Weight | ....................kg |

**Parent point:** Being able to tell the time is a skill that develops gradually throughout the primary school years. Practice and patience are vital. Involving children in measuring and weighing at home is another exciting skill for them to learn.

# Division

Sally Share is a teacher at Addington School. She is helping the children to get ready for a maths lesson.

The children are working in pairs.

Share these things between two children.

How many each?

10 ÷ 2 = ☐

How many each?

12 ÷ 2 = ☐

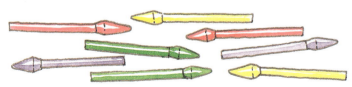

How many each?

2 ÷ 2 = ☐

How many each?

8 ÷ 2 = ☐

How many each?

6 ÷ 2 = ☐

Out in the playground the children are sharing their collections of toys so that they can play games.

Do you know how many things each child will have?

4 ÷ 2 = ☐

6 ÷ 3 = ☐

12 ÷ 3 = ☐

20 ÷ 4 = ☐

## Try your skills

Now try these divisions.

| | | |
|---|---|---|
| 9 ÷ 3 = ☐ | 30 ÷ 10 = ☐ |
| 16 ÷ 2 = ☐ | 18 ÷ 2 = ☐ |
| 6 ÷ 2 = ☐ | 5 ÷ 5 = ☐ |
| 20 ÷ 5 = ☐ | 14 ÷ 2 = ☐ |
| 12 ÷ 4 = ☐ | 30 ÷ 3 = ☐ |

*You're in the first division.*

**Parent point:** Children need plenty of practice in sharing out real objects.

# Odds and evens

Ossie Odd and Steven Even are each building a model. They are trying to share the blocks equally but sometimes there is one left over.

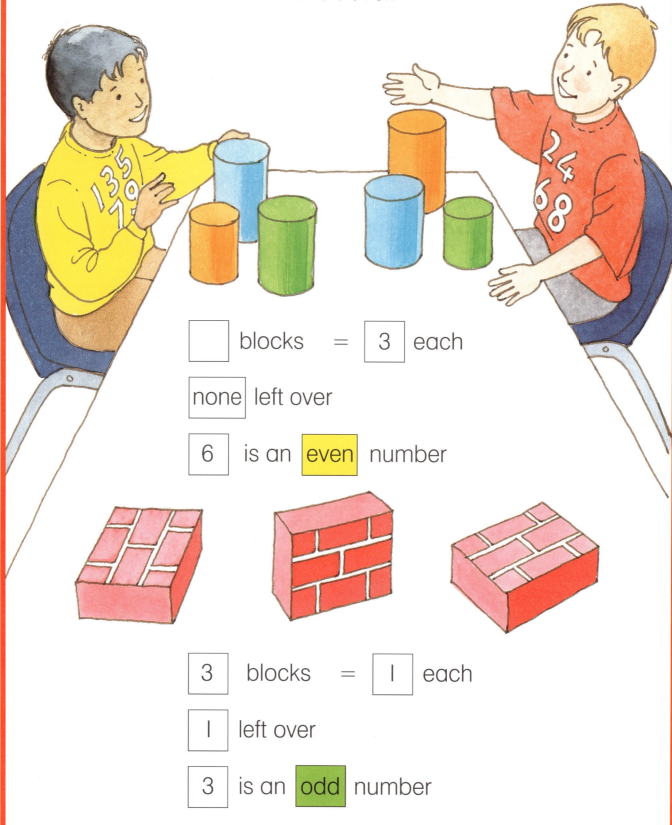

☐ blocks = 3 each

none left over

6 is an even number

3 blocks = 1 each

1 left over

3 is an odd number

Share the blocks and complete the charts.

☐ blocks = ☐ each
☐ left over
☐ is an ☐ number

☐ blocks = ☐ each
☐ left over
☐ is an ☐ number

☐ blocks = ☐ each
☐ left over
☐ is an ☐ number

☐ blocks = ☐ each
☐ left over
☐ is an ☐ number

☐ blocks = ☐ each
☐ left over
☐ is an ☐ number

*Even better!*

## Try your skills

Colour the **odd** numbers green and the **even** numbers yellow.

1  2  3  4  5  6  7  8  9  10
11  12  13  14  15  16  17  18  19  20

**Parent point:** When children understand the idea of odd and even, play counting games. Encourage them to count using the evens pattern (2, 4, 6, 8) and then the odds pattern (1, 3, 5, 7).

# Place value – hundreds, tens & units

The Score family like to play number building games.

They each pull 3 number cards from a hat and see which are the highest and lowest numbers they can build.

Here are some numbers they made.

|  |  | highest | lowest |
|---|---|---|---|
| Mr Score | 1  3  4 | 431 | 134 |
| Mrs Score | 6  2  3 | 632 | 236 |

Now help them to use these cards.

|  |  | highest | lowest |
|---|---|---|---|
| Sam Score | 1  4  1 | ___ | ___ |
| Sasha Score | 7  5  7 | ___ | ___ |
| Sue Score | 9  1  9 | ___ | ___ |

Do you know what the 2 means in these numbers?

Put a tick in the correct box.

2  3  1

3  2  1

| hundreds | tens | units |
|---|---|---|
|  |  |  |
|  |  |  |

Here are some numbers that the Score family have built.

Can you put them in order from lowest to highest?

| highest |
|---------|

144

134

199

236

411

413

577

633

775

991

| lowest |
|--------|

*Top score!*

## Try your skills

Look at these numbers and fill in the chart.

99
100
110
999
1000

| Thousands | Hundreds | Tens | Units |
|-----------|----------|------|-------|
|           |          |      |       |
|           |          |      |       |
|           |          |      |       |
|           |          |      |       |
|           |          |      |       |

**Parent point:** It is very important that children understand that a number can have a different value according to its position. Make some cards and play the game like the Score family.

# Mixed calculations

Lots of people are on their way home to Addington. Find the answer to the sum on each key. Do this for all the keys. Then match each one to its door.

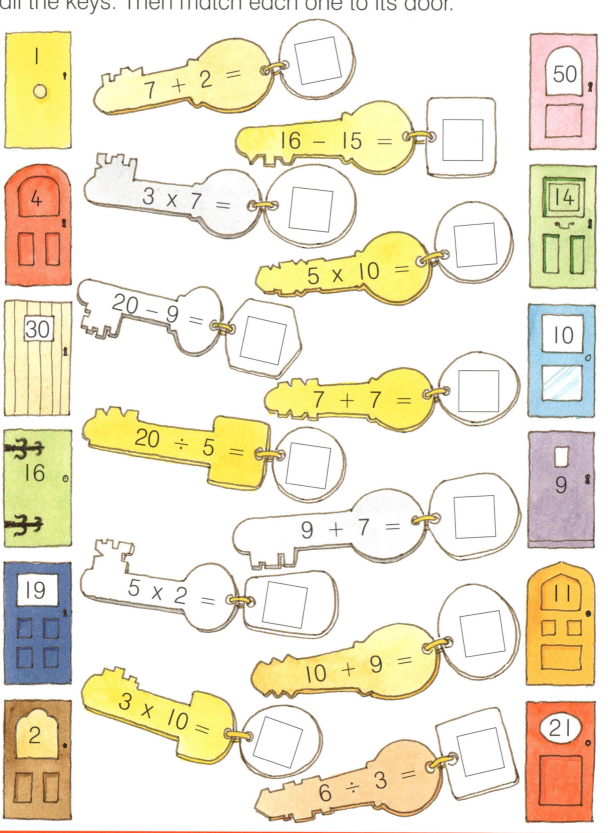

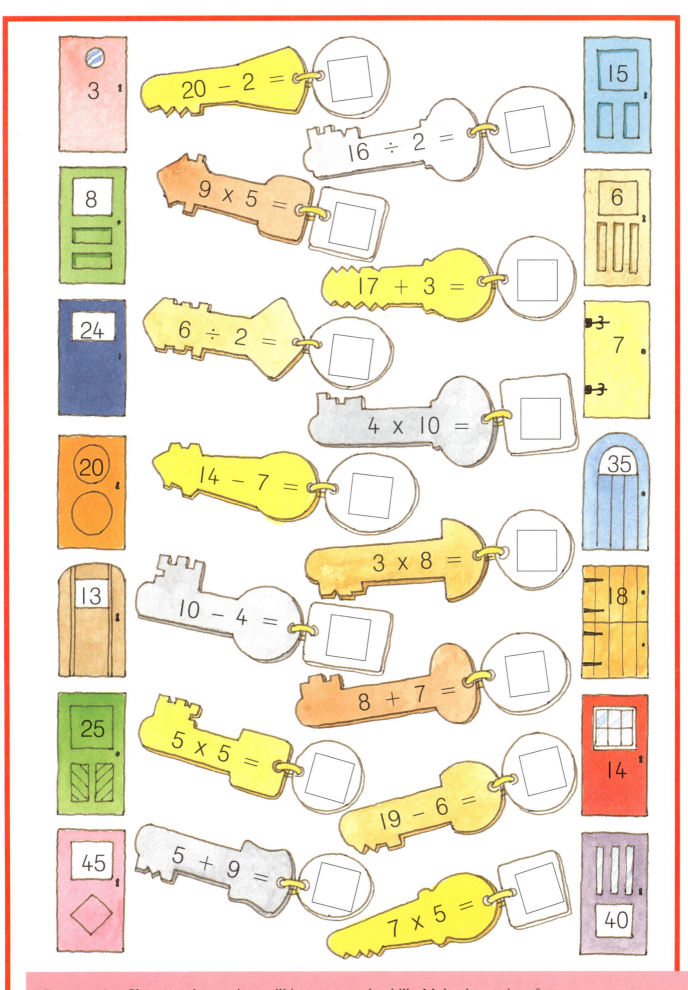

**Parent point:** Short regular sessions will improve maths skills. Make the sessions fun.

# Skills checklist

| page | | |
|---|---|---|
| 2 | Understands numbers 1–10 | ☐ |
| 3 | Can match numeral with appropriate number of items and sequence numbers 1–10 | ☐ |
| 4 | Understands role of estimating and importance of checking estimate | ☐ |
| 5 | Can estimate and check answers | ☐ |
| 6 | Can add to ten using pictorial aids | ☐ |
| 7 | Can add to ten using numerals | ☐ |
| 8 | Can subtract within 1–10 using pictorial aids | ☐ |
| 9 | Can subtract within 1–10 using numerals | ☐ |
| 10 | Understands grouping in tens with a remainder | ☐ |
| 11 | Understands that the position of a number shows its value. Can relate this to tens and units | ☐ |
| 12 | Understands concept of half or quarter of a whole item | ☐ |
| 13 | Understands concept of half or quarter of a number | ☐ |
| 14 | Understands the role of nought in subtraction | ☐ |
| 15 | Understands the role of nought in addition | ☐ |
| 16–17 | Can add to twenty | ☐ |
| 18 | Can work with money up to 25 pence using addition | ☐ |
| 19 | Can work with money up to 25 pence using subtraction | ☐ |
| 20 | Understands that multiplication is repeated addition | ☐ |
| 21 | Shows knowledge of x 2, x 3, x 4, x 5 and x 10 tables and multiplication facts up to 30 | ☐ |
| 22 | Can read a clock showing the hour, half hour or quarter hour | ☐ |
| 23 | Understands divisions on a measure or scale | ☐ |
| 24 | Understands the concept of division | ☐ |
| 25 | Can calculate divisions using picture aids and/or numerals alone | ☐ |
| 26 | Understands the concept of odd and even | ☐ |
| 27 | Can work out which numbers are odd or even | ☐ |
| 28 | Understands that the position of a number shows its value. Can relate this to hundreds, tens and units | ☐ |
| 29 | Can sequence numbers up to 1000 | ☐ |
| 30–31 | Can carry out a variety of basic calculations in addition, subtraction, multiplication and division | ☐ |